Name

Birth

Baptism

Our Family

Nihil obstat:
Rev. Timothy Hall, *Censor librorum*
September 4, 2017

Imprimatur:
†Most Rev. John M. Quinn, Bishop of Winona
September 4, 2017

Conceptual design and development by Jerry Windley-Daoust

Visual design and book build by Steve Nagel

Copy editing by Sibyl Niemann and Karen Carter

Cover image, *The Last Supper* by John August Swanson,
copyright 2009, Serigraph 23" by 30."
Used with permission: www.JohnAugustSwanson.com.

Acknowledgments continue on page 87.

Handbound edition by Jill Krase, Ovenbird Bindery

ISBN: 978-1-68192-514-1 (Inventory No. T2403)
LCCN: 2019939982

PRINTED IN THE UNITED STATES OF AMERICA

Our Sunday Visitor
Huntington, Indiana
www.osv.com

The Catholic Family Book of Prayers

A TREASURY OF PRAYERS
AND MEDITATIONS
FOR FAMILIES TO PRAY TOGETHER

Contents

Before You Pray 7

Morning Prayer 11

Basic Catholic Prayers 19

Prayers of Thanksgiving, Intercession, and Blessing 30

Prayers to Mary 44

Before You Pray

The call to prayer creates a threshold
between the ordinary activity of daily life
and the time of prayer. By it, we still ourselves, entering
that "inner room" (Matthew 6:6, NABRE) in which we
encounter the presence
of God.

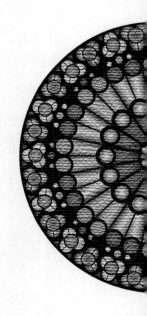

For me, prayer is a surge of the heart;
it is a simple look turned toward heaven,
it is a cry of recognition and of love.

—St. Thérèse of Lisieux

Call to Prayer
You may wish to use a bell or chimes
to gather family members for prayer.
Sound the bell (or verbally call to prayer)
about five minutes before your intended prayer time,
to allow family members time to transition.
Then use these simple words to call your family
to prayer. Follow with a period of silence
before beginning your prayer time.

Lasallian Practice of the Presence of God

LET us remember
that we are in the holy presence
of God.
   Silence.

Children's Call to Prayer

LET'S be as still as stones
and as silent as the stars
as we listen for the voice of God
whispering in our hearts.
   Silence.

St. Anselm's Call to Prayer

MAKE a little time for God and rest a while in him....
Speak now to God and say with your whole heart,
"I seek your face; your face, Lord, I desire."

Silence.

"Wherever we go, no matter how far off or how hidden from our eyes,
we will always find God and cannot escape the divine presence."
(St. John Baptist de La Salle)

Sign of the Cross

Use the Sign of the Cross to open and close your time of prayer.

IN THE NAME of the Father,
and of the Son,
and of the Holy Spirit.
Amen.

Touch your forehead on the word "Father,"
touch your chest on the word "Son,"
touch your left shoulder on the word "Holy,"
touch your right shoulder on the word "Spirit,"
and fold your hands on the word "Amen."

The Sign of the Cross invokes the Holy Trinity, recalls the Passion of
Christ, and affirms our willingness to take the cross upon ourselves.
Tertullian, one of the Church Fathers, suggests that the Sign of the
Cross be made frequently to sanctify the activities of the day: "When
we put on our clothes and shoes, when we bathe, when we sit at table,
when we light the lamps, on couch, on seat, in all the ordinary actions
of daily life, we trace upon the forehead the sign."

The Triple Sign of the Cross

Make the Triple Sign of the Cross before reading or hearing the Holy Scriptures. Use the thumb of the right hand to trace a small cross on your forehead, lips, and heart as you silently pray:

M AY the Word of God ever be on my mind, on my lips, and in my heart.

The Triple Sign of the Cross is the gesture we make at Mass when the lector says, "A reading from the Holy Gospel according to…" to which we respond, "Glory to you, O Lord," while simultaneously crossing ourselves.

Morning Prayer

*St. Paul urged his readers to "pray constantly"
(1 Thessalonians 5:17). Over the centuries,
the Church developed a way to pray at regular
intervals throughout the day. This traditional
practice is known as the Liturgy of the Hours,
or the Divine Office. The Liturgy of the Hours
is like an extension of the celebration of Mass
into everyday life, a way for Christians to
sanctify
the day.*

*Morning Prayer, also called Lauds, is one of the
major "hours" in the Liturgy of the Hours. While
it may be impractical to formally pray the full
Office daily, many families "bookend" their day
with morning and evening prayers.*

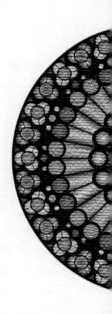

*The following morning prayers offer a simple way
for your family to call to mind the divine presence
at the beginning of the day, and to offer that day
to God.*

A Short Morning Offering for Children

Thank you, God, for giving us this day;
help us to be like Jesus in all we think, do, and say.

Amen.

Canticle of Zechariah (Benedictus)

BLESSED be the Lord, the God of Israel,
   for he has visited and brought redemption to his people.
He has raised up a horn for our salvation
   within the house of David his servant,
even as he promised through the mouth of his holy prophets
   from of old:
salvation from our enemies and from the hand
of all who hate us,
to show mercy to our fathers
   and to be mindful of his holy covenant
and of the oath he swore
to Abraham our father,
and to grant us that,
   rescued from the hand of enemies,

   without fear we might worship him
     in holiness and righteousness
      before him all our days.
And you, child, will be called prophet
     of the Most High,
      for you will go before the Lord to
     prepare his ways,

to give his people knowledge of salvation
    through the forgiveness of their sins,
because of the tender mercy of our God
    by which the daybreak from on high will visit us
to shine on those who sit in darkness and death's shadow,
    to guide our feet into the path of peace.

Glory be to the Father,
and to the Son,
and to the Holy Spirit:
as it was in the beginning,
is now, and will be forever.

Amen.

The Canticle of Zechariah is taken from the song that Zechariah sings after regaining his voice at the birth of his son, John (Luke 1:68-79, NABRE). It was adopted for Morning Prayer by St. Benedict in the sixth century, possibly because of the reference to the dawn, and it is one of the central prayers of the Divine Office.

Angel of God

ANGEL of God, my guardian dear,
to whom God's love commits me here:
ever this day be at my side,
to light, to guard, to rule, and guide.
Amen.

"Already here on earth the Christian life shares by faith in the blessed company of angels and men united in God." (*Catechism of the Catholic Church* 336)

Morning Offering

O JESUS, through the Immaculate Heart of Mary,
I offer you my prayers, works, joys,
and sufferings of this day
for all the intentions of your Sacred Heart,
in union with the Holy Sacrifice of the Mass
throughout the world,
for the salvation of souls,
the reparation of sins,
the reunion of all Christians,
and in particular for the intentions
of the Holy Father this month.

Amen.

This prayer was written in 1844 by Fr. François-Xavier Gautrelet, S.J., one of the founders of the Apostleship of Prayer, as a way for Christians to make a daily offering of themselves to the Lord. You can find the pope's monthly prayer intentions at apostleshipofprayer. org.

This Is the Day the Lord Has Made
(Psalm 118:24)

THIS is the day that the Lord has made;
let us be glad and rejoice in it.

Psalm 118 is from a thanksgiving liturgy in which the king, priests, and all the people processed into the temple to give thanks for deliverance from enemies.

Prayer of Saint Francis

LORD, make me an instrument of your peace;
where there is hatred, let me sow love;
where there is injury, pardon;
where there is error, truth;
where there is doubt, faith;
where there is despair, hope;
where there is darkness, light;
and where there is sadness, joy.

O Divine Master, grant that I may not so much seek
to be consoled as to console;
to be understood as to understand;
to be loved as to love.
For it is in giving that we receive;
it is in pardoning that we are pardoned;
and it is in dying that we are born to eternal life.
✠

How would your family life look different
if you put this prayer into practice today?

Although this prayer was written in the spirit of St. Francis, it first
appeared in a small French church magazine, *The Little Bell*, in 1912.
It was widely distributed during World War I and World War II.

Lorica of St. Patrick

I ARISE today through
God's strength to pilot me,
God's might to uphold me,
God's wisdom to guide me,
God's eye to see before me,
God's ear to hear me,
God's word to speak for me,
God's hand to guard me,
God's way to lie before me,
God's shield to protect me,
God's host to secure me—
against snares of devils,
against temptations and vices,
against inclinations of nature,
against everyone who shall wish me ill,
whether far or near,
alone and in a crowd . . .

Christ, be with me,
Christ before me,
Christ behind me,
Christ in me,
Christ beneath me,
Christ above me,

Christ on my right,
Christ on my left,
Christ where I lie,
Christ where I sit,
Christ where I arise,
Christ in the heart of every man who thinks of me,
Christ in the mouth of every man who speaks of me,
Christ in every eye that sees me,
Christ in every ear that hears me.

Salvation is of the Lord.
Salvation is of the Lord.
Salvation is of the Christ.
May your salvation, O Lord,
be ever with us.

Amen.

The Lorica of St. Patrick, traditionally attributed to the saint, may have been composed long after his time. *Lorica* means "breastplate" or "armor" in Latin; loricas were prayers for protection, developed within the monastic tradition. St. Patrick's Lorica has taken many forms over the years; this is one of the shorter versions.

Pied Beauty

GLORY be to God for dappled things—
  For skies of couple-colour as a brinded cow;
    For rose-moles all in stipple upon trout that swim;
Fresh-firecoal chestnut-falls; finches' wings;
  Landscape plotted and pieced—fold, fallow, and plough;
    And all trades, their gear and tackle and trim.
All things counter, original, spare, strange;
  Whatever is fickle, freckled (who knows how?)
    With swift, slow; sweet, sour; adazzle, dim;
He fathers-forth whose beauty is past change:
                Praise Him.

The author of this poem, Gerard Manley Hopkins, was a Jesuit priest whose unusual poetry was rejected by publishers during his lifetime. He burned all of his poetry upon entering the Society of Jesus as an act of humility, but eventually came to see his poetry as consistent with his vocation. Today, he is hailed as "one of the three or four greatest poets of the Victorian era" by the Poetry Foundation.

Basic Catholic Prayers

The following prayers are among the most popular in the Church, and most are known "by heart" by most practicing Catholics. The best way for children to memorize them is to recite them often.

Prayer is the raising of the mind to God. We must always remember this. The actual words matter less.

—St. Pope John XXIII

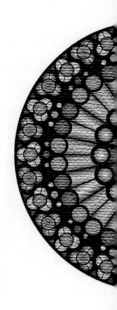

Even if we speak with a low voice, even if we whisper without opening the lips, even if we call to him only from the depths of our heart, our unspoken word always reaches God, and God always listens.

—St. Clement of Alexandria

You go to pray; to become a bonfire, a living flame, giving light and heat.

—St. Josemaria Escriva

The Apostles' Creed

I BELIEVE in God,
the Father almighty,
Creator of heaven and earth,
and in Jesus Christ, his only Son, our Lord,
who was conceived by the Holy Spirit,
born of the Virgin Mary,
suffered under Pontius Pilate,
was crucified, died and was buried;
he descended into hell;
on the third day he rose again from the dead;
he ascended into heaven,
and is seated at the right hand of God the Father almighty;
from there he will come to judge the living and the dead.

I believe in the Holy Spirit,
the holy catholic Church,
the communion of saints,
the forgiveness of sins,
the resurrection of the body,
and life everlasting.

Amen.

The Apostles' Creed is trinitarian, affirming belief in the Father, Son, and the Holy Spirit. It is one of the oldest Christian creeds (statements of belief), and is the basis for the longer Nicene Creed that we say at Mass.

For another way to appreciate and pray the Apostles' Creed, try meditating on one line at a time over the course of twenty days. A large portion of the *Catechism of the Catholic Church* (199–1065) explains each of the statements of the Creed in detail.

The Lord's Prayer (Our Father)

OUR FATHER who art in heaven,
hallowed be thy name.
Thy kingdom come,
thy will be done on earth
as it is in heaven.
Give us this day our daily bread,
and forgive us our trespasses,
as we forgive those
who trespass against us,
and lead us not into temptation,
but deliver us from evil.

Amen.

Try praying the Lord's Prayer very slowly as a form of meditation; it may also be chanted. See Catechism *2759–2865 for a beautiful reflection on the significance of the Lord's Prayer.*

The Lord's Prayer is the prayer that Jesus taught to his disciples (see Matthew 6:9–13 and Luke 11:2–4). Quoting Tertullian, the *Catechism* says that it is "truly a summary of the whole Gospel" and the foundation of all further prayer (2761).

Hail Mary

HAIL Mary, full of grace,
the Lord is with thee;
blessed art thou among women,
and blessed is the fruit of thy womb, Jesus.
Holy Mary, Mother of God,
pray for us sinners,
now and at the hour of our death.

Amen.

The Hail Mary is based on the greeting of Mary by the angel Gabriel (Luke 1:28) and by Elizabeth (Luke 1:42). The prayer then affirms Mary as the "mother of God," and asks her to pray to her Son on our behalf. We pray for her to watch over us at the hour of our death just as she watched over her Son at the hour of his death. See *Catechism* 2673–2679 for a reflection on the significance of this prayer.

Glory Be to the Father (Lesser Doxology)

GLORY to the Father,
and to the Son,
and to the Holy Spirit:
as it was in the beginning,
is now, and ever shall be, world without end.

Amen.

A doxology is a short verse praising God. The "Glory Be" is often used in conjunction with other prayers, especially in the Liturgy of the Hours and the Rosary.

Gloria in Excelsis Deo (Great Doxology)

GLORY to God in the highest,
and on earth peace to people of good will.
We praise you,
we bless you,
we adore you,
we glorify you,
we give you thanks for your great glory,
Lord God, heavenly King,
O God, almighty Father.
Lord Jesus Christ, Only Begotten Son,
Lord God, Lamb of God, Son of the Father,
you take away the sins of the world,
have mercy on us;
you take away the sins of the world,
receive our prayer;
you are seated at the right hand of the Father,
have mercy on us.
For you alone are the Holy One,
you alone are the Lord,
you alone are the Most High,
Jesus Christ,
with the Holy Spirit,
in the glory of God the Father.

Amen.

This hymn of praise dates to the earliest centuries of the Church, and is sung at Mass on Sundays outside of Advent and Lent and on holy days.

Confiteor (I Confess)

I CONFESS to almighty God
and to you, my brothers and sisters,
that I have greatly sinned,
in my thoughts and in my words,
in what I have done and in what I have failed to do,
through my fault, through my fault,
through my most grievous fault;
therefore I ask blessed Mary ever-Virgin,
all the Angels and Saints,
and you, my brothers and sisters,
to pray for me to the Lord our God.
✠

The Confiteor is one of three forms of the Penitential Act that may be said at the beginning of Mass. It is a form of general confession, and in the context of the Mass, offers absolution for venial sins.

Come, Holy Spirit

COME, Holy Spirit, fill the hearts of your faithful,
and kindle in them the fire of your love.
Send forth your Spirit and they shall be created.
And you will renew the face of the earth.

Lord,
by the light of the Holy Spirit
you have taught the hearts of your faithful.
In the same Spirit
help us to relish what is right
and always rejoice
in your consolation.
We ask this through Christ
our Lord.

Amen.

"'No one can say "Jesus is Lord" except by the Holy Spirit' (1 Corinthians 12:3). Every time we begin to pray to Jesus it is the Holy Spirit who draws us on the way of prayer by his prevenient grace. Since he teaches us to pray by recalling Christ, how could we not pray to the Spirit too? That is why the Church invites us to call upon the Holy Spirit every day, especially at the beginning and the end of every important action." (*Catechism* 2670)

Te Deum Laudamus (God, We Praise You)

YOU are God: we praise you;
you are the Lord: we acclaim you;
you are the eternal Father:
all creation worships you.
To you all angels, all the powers of heaven,
Cherubim and Seraphim, sing in endless praise:
Holy, holy, holy, Lord,
God of power and might,
heaven and earth are full of your glory.
The glorious company of apostles praise you.
The noble fellowship of prophets praise you.
The white-robed army of martyrs praise you.
Throughout the world
the holy Church acclaims you:
Father, of majesty unbounded,
your true and only Son,
worthy of all worship,
and the Holy Spirit,
advocate and guide.
You, Christ, are the king
of glory, the eternal Son
of the Father.

When you became man to set us free
you did not spurn the Virgin's womb.
You overcame the sting of death,
and opened the kingdom of heaven
to all believers.
You are seated at God's right hand in glory.
We believe that you will come, and
be our judge.
Come then, Lord, and help your people,
bought with the price of your own blood,
and bring us with your saints
to glory everlasting.
Save your people, Lord, and bless
your inheritance.
Govern and uphold them now and always.
Day by day we bless you.
We praise your name forever.
Keep us today, Lord, from all sin.
Have mercy on us, Lord, have mercy.
Lord, show us your love and mercy;
for we put our trust in you.
In you, Lord, is our hope:
and we shall never hope in vain.

✠

This fifth-century hymn of praise is sung or recited as part of the
Liturgy of the Hours, and at times of thanksgiving for a special blessing.

Anima Christi

SOUL of Christ make me holy;
Body of Christ save me;
Blood of Christ fill me with love;
Water from Christ's side, wash me;
Passion of Christ strengthen me.
O Good Jesus hear me;
within your wounds hide me.
Never let me be parted from you;
from the evil enemy protect me;
at the hour of my death call,
and tell me to come to you,
that with your saints and angels
I may praise you
forever and ever.

Amen.

This prayer, which dates to the early fourteenth century, traditionally is prayed after receiving the Eucharist. St. Ignatius of Loyola included it at the beginning of his Spiritual Exercises.

Prayer to St. Michael

ST. MICHAEL the Archangel,
defend us in battle;
be our protection against the wickedness
and snares of the devil.
May God rebuke him, we humbly pray:
and do thou, O prince of the heavenly host,
by the power of God,
thrust into hell Satan and all the evil spirits
who prowl about the world seeking the ruin of souls.

Amen.

This prayer of Pope Leo XIII, originally intended to be said after Mass, was written to ask for God's help restoring the sovereignty of the pope after Rome was lost to Italy, a situation that was resolved with the creation of the Vatican State in 1929.

Today, the prayer is said to ask for protection from evil. It is sometimes said with children before bedtime as a petition for peaceful sleep.

Prayers of Thanksgiving, Intercession, and Blessing

Here you will find prayers of thanksgiving, intercession, and blessing to use during your family prayer time, or at any time throughout the day.

We must speak to God
as a friend speaks to his friend,
   servant to his master;
      now asking some favor,
        now acknowledging our faults,
        and communicating to Him all that
        concerns us:
        our thoughts, our fears,
        our projects, our desires,
       and in all things seeking
       His counsel.
—St. Ignatius of Loyola

Consecration to the Holy Family

JESUS, Mary, and Joseph,
we place our family under your care
and at your service.

Jesus,
you taught that all those
who do the will of your Father in heaven
are your family.
Strengthen us to do your Father's will
so we might become a true family
to one another,
and to all people of good will.

Mary,
you said "yes" to God
with all your heart, all your soul,
all your mind, and all your strength;
and by your "yes,"
you gave birth to the Son of God.
Help us to say "yes" to God every day
so that we, too, might bring Jesus
into the world.

Joseph,
you listened to God's voice
in your work, in your prayer,
and in your dreams;
help us to hear God's voice
so that, like you, we might
rise from our sleep
to do the will of God.

Jesus, Mary, and Joseph, pray for our family,
and send down upon us the help of the Holy Spirit:
bless our home with peace and joy,
and give us
kindness and gentleness,
courage and humility,
strength and self-control,
mercy and forgiveness,
patience and generosity;
and most of all, give us your love,
that we might share it with one another,
and the whole world.

Amen.

Intercessory Prayers

Invite family members to offer intentions for prayer. These intentions can be written out in advance and then read aloud by the prayer leader, or spoken out loud spontaneously in the course of the time of prayer. In either case, use the following formula.

*L*EADER: **For** *(name of your intention)*, **let us pray to the Lord.**

Response: **Lord, hear our prayer.**

Other possible responses:
Lord, have mercy.
Word of God, lead us.
Be our help, O Lord.

Intentions

   If you need inspiration for intentions, consider this list:

For forgiveness and healing for all the times we hurt ourselves, others, and God by our sins today, let us pray. *(Response)*

For love, respect, and peace to reign in our family, that our life together might be a witness to others of God's loving presence, let us pray. *(Response)*

For the Church, especially for the pope, our bishop, *(name),* **our pastor,** *(name),* **all those who work in the Church, and Christians everywhere: that they may faithfully carry on the mission of Jesus in the world, let us pray.** *(Response)*

For those in positions of leadership, especially *(name),* that they might lead with wisdom and always seek the common good, let us pray. *(Response)*

For those who are lonely, sick, or imprisoned; for the victims of violence and injustice; and for those who do not have what they need to live as fully as God intended, let us pray. *(Response)*

In thanksgiving for God's many blessings on our family, let us pray. *(Response)*

"Since Abraham, intercession—asking on behalf of another—has been characteristic of a heart attuned to God's mercy. In the age of the Church, Christian intercession participates in Christ's, as an expression of the communion of saints. In intercession, he who prays looks 'not only to his own interests, but also to the interests of others,' even to the point of praying for those who do him harm (Philippians 2:4; cf. Acts 7:60; Luke 23:28, 34)." *(Catechism* 2635)

Let Nothing Disturb You

LET nothing disturb you.
Let nothing frighten you.
All things are passing away;
God never changes.
Patience obtains all things.
Whoever has God lacks nothing;
God alone suffices.

St. Teresa of Avila wrote this meditative prayer in the sixteenth century and carried it in her prayer book, which is why it is sometimes called "St. Teresa's Bookmark."

Giving Thanks

Before praying this prayer, recollect the day as a family. Then invite each family member to respond to the invitation to give thanks, as each is moved.

*L*EADER: **For what should we thank God today?**

After each statement of gratitude, all respond with one of the following verses:

Psalm 9:1

I will give thanks to the Lord
with my whole heart;
I will tell of all
your wonderful deeds.

Psalm 30:4

Sing praises to the Lord,
O you his faithful ones,
and give thanks to his holy name.
Psalm 118:1

O give thanks to the Lord,
for he is good;
his steadfast love endures forever!

1 Corinthians 15:57
Thanks be to God,
who gives us the victory
through our Lord Jesus Christ.

"Rejoice always, pray without ceasing, give thanks in all circumstances; for this is the will of God in Christ Jesus for you." (Thessalonians 5:16–18)

Canticle of the Sun (A Song of St. Francis)

MOST high, all powerful, all good Lord!
All praise is yours, all glory, all honor, and all blessing.

To you alone, Most High, do they belong.
No mortal lips are worthy to pronounce your name.

Be praised, my Lord, through all your creatures,
especially through my lord Brother Sun,
who brings the day; and you give light through him.
And he is beautiful and radiant in all his splendor!
Of you, Most High, he bears the likeness.

Be praised, my Lord, through Sister Moon and the stars;
in the heavens you have made them bright,
precious and beautiful.

Be praised, my Lord, through Brothers Wind and Air,
and clouds and storms, and all the weather,
through which you give your creatures sustenance.

Be praised, my Lord, through Sister Water;
she is very useful, and humble, and precious, and pure.

Be praised, my Lord, through Brother Fire,
through whom you brighten
the night.
He is beautiful and cheerful, and powerful and strong.

Be praised, my Lord,
   through our sister Mother Earth,
   who feeds us and rules us,
   and produces various fruits
   with colored flowers and herbs.

Be praised, my Lord, through those
who forgive for love of You;
through those who endure sickness and trial.

Happy those who endure in peace,
for by you, Most High, they will be crowned.

Be praised, my Lord, through our sister Bodily Death,
from whose embrace no living person can escape.
Woe to those who die in mortal sin!
Happy those she finds doing your most holy will.
The second death can do no harm to them.

Praise and bless my Lord, and give thanks,
and serve him with great humility.

This hymn of thanksgiving was composed by St. Francis in 1224.
The last verse is said to have been added while Francis lay on his
deathbed two years later.

Simple Blessings

Every baptized person is called both to be a blessing and to bless (Catechism 1669). Blessings generally have three parts: praise of God; a request for God's gifts; and the invocation of the name of Jesus while making the Sign of the Cross. The following formulas may be used to bless people or objects. For blessings suggested by the Church for specific times and purposes, see Catholic Household Blessings and Prayers, *edited and published by the United States Conference of Catholic Bishops.*

Blessing of Persons

Bless family members and other persons for special times and purposes, such as sickness, the start of an endeavor, or sleep.

LEADER: **Our help is in the name of the Lord . . .**

All: **. . . who has made heaven and earth.**

Leader: **Blessed is the name of the Lord.**

All: **Now and forever.**

   Optionally, an appropriate Scripture reading or verse may be read at this time.

Leader: **Let us pray.**
O God, by whose Word all things are made holy,
pour forth your blessing upon *(name of the person).*
Grant him/her *(name of the desired gift or blessing, e.g., health, strength, safe journey, etc.)***, that he/she may serve you.**
   Make the Sign of the Cross on the person being blessed.
We ask this through Christ our Lord.

All: **Amen.**

Blessing of an Object

*L*EADER: Our help is in the name of the Lord . . .

All: . . . who has made heaven and earth.

Leader: Blessed is the name of the Lord.

All: Now and forever.

Optionally, an appropriate Scripture reading or verse may be read at this time.

Leader: Let us pray.

O God, by whose Word all things are made holy,
pour forth your blessing upon *(name of the object)*,
and grant that whoever shall use it
with thanksgiving, according to your law and will,
may receive from you *(name of the good desired, e.g., successful studies, a plentiful harvest, etc.).*
We ask this through Christ our Lord.

All: Amen.

Blessing for Someone Who Is Sick

*L*EADER: Our help is in the name of the Lord . . .

Response: . . . who has made heaven and earth.

Leader: Let us listen to these words from the Gospel according to Luke:

> As the sun was setting, all those who had any who were sick with various kinds of diseases brought them to him; and he laid his hands on each of them and cured them. The Gospel of the Lord.

Response: Praise to you, Lord Jesus Christ.

Leader: Lord Jesus, as you once laid your hands on the sick, we ask you now to send your healing Spirit
onto *(name of the person)*:
comfort and strengthen him/her,
free him/her from all illness,
and restore him/her to health.

> *The prayer leader makes the Sign of the Cross on the forehead of the sick person.*

We ask this in the name of the Father, and the Son, and the Holy Spirit.

Response: Amen.

"Prayer is by nature a dialogue and a union of man with God; its effect is to hold the world together, for it achieves a reconciliation with God." *(St. John Climacus)*

Aaron's Blessing

MAY the Lord bless you and keep you.
Response: Amen.

May his face shine upon you, and be gracious to you.
Response: Amen.

May he look upon you with kindness, and give you his peace.
Response: Amen.

May almighty God bless you,
the Father, and the Son, and the Holy Spirit.

Response: Amen.

This blessing is called the Aaronic Blessing or the Priestly Blessing because it is the blessing that God gave to Aaron for the blessing of the people of Israel; you can find it in Numbers 6:22–27.

Eternal Rest

ETERNAL rest grant unto him/her, O Lord;
and let perpetual light shine upon him/her.
May he/she rest in peace.

Amen.

This prayer is often said when visiting or passing cemeteries, or upon learning of someone's death; it is also prayed between decades of the rosary during the month of November.

"From the beginning the Church has honored the memory of the dead and offered prayers in suffrage for them...." (*Catechism* 1032)

Bless Us, O Lord

BLESS us, O Lord,
and these your gifts
which we are about to receive
from your bounty,
through Christ, our Lord.

Amen.

Come, Lord Jesus

COME, Lord Jesus,
be our guest;
let these gifts
to us be blessed.

Amen.

For Food, Faith, and Friends

FOR food in a world where many walk in hunger;
For faith in a world where many walk in fear;
For friends in a world where many walk alone;
We give you thanks, O Lord.

Blessed Are You, Lord

BLESSED are you, Lord our God,
maker of heaven and earth
and Father of all your people:
we give you glory for your goodness
and for your loving care for us.

Bless this food [this bread]
and grant that all who eat it
may be strong in body
and grow in your love.

Blessed are you, Lord our God,
for ever and ever.

Grace after Meals

LORD God,
for our food we thank you,
for our joys we praise you,
for our life we glorify you.
Help us to love you more.
Amen.

"As they gather at table and see in the food they share a sign of God's blessings on them, Christians should be mindful of the poor, who lack even the bare minimum of food that those at table may have in abundance. By their moderation they will therefore try to provide help for the hungry and as a sign of Christ's love will on occasion invite the poor to their own table, in keeping with the words of Christ recorded in the Gospel (*see Luke 14:13–14*)." (*Book of Blessings*, #1030–1031)

Prayers to Mary

Why do Catholics venerate Mary and ask for her intercession in prayer? Through Mary, God invited the human race to cooperate in his plan of salvation. When she said "yes" to that invitation, Mary reversed the "no" of Adam and Eve. And by saying "yes" to God's desire to live within her, she became the prototype of all Christians. Like Mary, when we say "yes" to cooperating with God, he lives within us—especially through the sacraments of baptism and the Holy Eucharist, by which God "becomes flesh" through us. This is why the Church points to Mary as the model Christian.

Although our understanding of Mary's role in the mystery of salvation has developed over the centuries, devotion to Mary has historical roots that go back to the writings of the early Church, not to mention the Scriptures. Mary is "favored" by God and "blessed among women," according to the angel Gabriel (Luke 1:28), because of the role she plays in fulfilling God's plan of salvation. Moreover, Jesus appointed her as our "spiritual mother" (John 19:27).

Besides the prayers here, see also the Hail Mary (page 22) and the Canticle of Mary (page 78).

Regina Caeli

*L*EADER: Queen of Heaven, rejoice, alleluia.

Response: For he whom you did merit to bear, alleluia.

Leader: Has risen, as he said, alleluia.

Response: Pray for us to God, alleluia.

Leader: Rejoice and be glad, O Virgin Mary, alleluia.

Response: For the Lord has truly risen, alleluia.

Leader: Let us pray. O God, who gave joy to the world through the resurrection of thy Son, our Lord Jesus Christ, grant we beseech thee, that through the intercession of the Virgin Mary, his mother, we may obtain the joys of everlasting life. Through the same Christ our Lord.

Amen.

Regina Caeli is Latin for "Queen of Heaven." (It's pronounced rej-EE-na KAY-lee.) This prayer replaces the Angelus during the Easter season.

Angelus

*L*EADER: The angel of the Lord declared unto Mary.

Response: And she conceived of the Holy Spirit.

Hail, Mary, full of grace,
the Lord is with thee;
blessed art thou among women,
and blessed is the fruit of thy womb, Jesus.
Holy Mary, Mother of God,
pray for us sinners,
now and at the hour of our death.

Leader: Behold the handmaid of the Lord.

Response: Be it done unto me according to thy Word.

Hail, Mary, full of grace.... *(Pray the Hail Mary again.)*

Leader: And the Word was made flesh.

Response: And dwelt amongst us.

Hail, Mary, full of grace.... *(Pray the Hail Mary again.)*

Leader: Pray for us, O Holy Mother of God.

Response: That we may be made worthy of the promises of Christ.

Leader: Let us pray. Pour forth, we beseech thee, O Lord, thy grace into our hearts, that we to whom the incarnation of Christ thy Son was made known by the message of an angel, may by his passion and cross be brought to the glory of his resurrection; through the same Christ our Lord.

Response: Amen.

The Angelus (so named because "angel" is the first word) commemorates the Incarnation, and is traditionally prayed at 6 a.m., noon, and 6 p.m. During the Easter season, it is replaced by the Regina Caeli.

Fiat (Luke 1:38)

HERE am I, the servant of the Lord;
let it be with me according to your word.

This prayer is taken from Mary's response to the angel Gabriel's announcement that she had been chosen to give birth to the Son of God. The *Catechism of the Catholic Church* says of Mary's *fiat*: "This is Christian prayer: to be wholly God's, because he is wholly ours." (2617)

Memorare

REMEMBER, O most gracious Virgin Mary,
that never was it known that anyone who fled
to thy protection, implored thy help, or sought
thine intercession was left unaided.

Inspired by this confidence, I fly unto thee,
O Virgin of virgins, my mother; to thee do I come,
before thee I stand, sinful and sorrowful.

O Mother of the Word Incarnate, despise not my petitions,
but in thy mercy hear and answer me.

Amen.

This prayer dates to the fifteenth century but was popularized by St. Claude Bernard (1588–1641), a priest dedicated to prisoners and criminals condemned to death. He used this prayer extensively in his work, distributing hundreds of thousands of copies wherever he felt the prayer would do some good.

Litany of Loreto

This prayer is prayed antiphonally (the prayer leader says the first part, then all respond with the second part). The response is set in italics.

LORD, have mercy.
Christ, have mercy.

Lord, have mercy. Christ, hear us.
Christ, graciously hear us.

God, the Father of heaven,
have mercy on us.

God the Son, Redeemer of the world,
have mercy on us.

God the Holy Spirit,
have mercy on us.

Holy Trinity, one God,
have mercy on us.

Holy Mary, *pray for us.*
Holy Mother of God, *pray for us.*
Holy Virgin of virgins, *pray for us.*
Mother of Christ, *pray for us.*
Mother of the Church, *pray for us.*
Mother of divine grace, *pray for us.*
Mother most pure, *pray for us.*
Mother most chaste, *pray for us.*
Mother inviolate, *pray for us.*
Mother undefiled, *pray for us.*
Mother most amiable, *pray for us.*
Mother most admirable, *pray for us.*
Mother of good counsel, *pray for us.*
Mother of our Creator, *pray for us.*
Mother of our Savior, *pray for us.*
Virgin most prudent, *pray for us.*
Virgin most venerable, *pray for us.*

48

Virgin most renowned, *pray for us.*
Virgin most powerful, *pray for us.*
Virgin most merciful, *pray for us.*
Virgin most faithful, *pray for us.*
Mirror of justice, *pray for us.*
Seat of wisdom, *pray for us.*
Cause of our joy, *pray for us.*
Spiritual vessel, *pray for us.*
Vessel of honor, pray for us.
Singular vessel of devotion, *pray for us.*
Mystical rose, *pray for us.*
Tower of David, *pray for us.*
Tower of ivory, *pray for us.*
House of gold, *pray for us.*
Ark of the covenant, *pray for us.*
Gate of heaven, *pray for us.*
Morning star, *pray for us.*
Health of the sick, *pray for us.*
Refuge of sinners, *pray for us.*
Comforter of the afflicted, *pray for us.*
Help of Christians, *pray for us.*
Queen of angels, *pray for us.*
Queen of patriarchs, *pray for us.*
Queen of prophets, *pray for us.*
Queen of apostles, *pray for us.*
Queen of martyrs, *pray for us.*
Queen of confessors, *pray for us.*
Queen of virgins, *pray for us.*
Queen of all saints, *pray for us.*
Queen conceived without original sin, *pray for us.*
Queen assumed into heaven, *pray for us.*
Queen of the most holy Rosary, *pray for us.*
Queen of families, *pray for us.*
Queen of peace, *pray for us.*

Lamb of God, you take away sins of the world;
spare us, O Lord.

Lamb of God, you take away the sins of the world;
graciously hear us, O Lord.

Lamb of God, you take away the sins of the world;
have mercy on us.

Pray for us, O Holy Mother of God,
that we may be made worthy of the promises of Christ.

Let us pray:
Grant, we beg you, O Lord God,
that we your servants
may enjoy lasting health of mind and body,
and by the glorious intercession
of the Blessed Mary, ever Virgin,
be delivered from present sorrow
and enter into the joy of eternal happiness.
Through Christ our Lord.

Amen.

The Litany of Loreto was composed in the sixteenth century at the Shrine of Our Lady of Loreto in Italy. The shrine is said to contain the house in which the Blessed Virgin lived, and is a major pilgrimage site.

Fatima Prayer

O MY Jesus,
forgive us our sins,
save us from the fires of hell;
lead all souls to Heaven,
especially those in most need of your mercy.

In 1917, the Blessed Virgin Mary appeared to three children in Fatima, Portugal, over a period of many months. According to the children, Mary requested that this prayer be said as part of the Rosary, which is why many Catholics add it to the end of each decade.

Hail, Holy Queen (Salve Regina)

HAIL, holy Queen, Mother of Mercy,
hail our life, our sweetness and our hope.

To thee do we cry, poor banished children of Eve;
to thee do we send up our sighs,
mourning and weeping in this valley of tears.

Turn then, most gracious advocate,
thine eyes of mercy toward us;
and after this our exile,
show unto us the blessed fruit of thy womb, Jesus.

O clement, O loving, O sweet Virgin Mary…

Leader: …pray for us, O holy Mother of God…

Response: …that we may be made worthy of the promises
of Christ.

Amen.

This prayer is typically said as part of the Liturgy of the Hours during the last prayers of the day, and also as the final prayer of the Rosary.

The Rosary

HOW TO PRAY THE ROSARY

Rosary beads are not necessary to pray the Rosary, but they are traditional; the beads add a tactile dimension to the prayer that reflects the sacramental, incarnational sensibility of Catholic faith.

Usually, when the Rosary is prayed in a group setting, one person leads by saying the first half of the Apostles' Creed and each Our Father, Hail Mary, and Glory Be, while the entire group says the second half of each prayer.

1. Holding the crucifix, make the Sign of the Cross (page 9).

2. Then say the Apostles' Creed (page 20).

3. On the first large bead above the crucifix, say an Our Father (page 21). On each of the next three smaller beads, pray a Hail Mary. (page 22) (Traditionally, these are prayed for the intention of an increase of faith, hope, and charity.)

4. Pray the Glory Be (page 22). The main part of the Rosary is divided up into five "decades," or sets of ten small beads. A different mystery of the rosary is contemplated during each decade. A decade of the rosary is prayed as follows:

5. Announce the mystery of the rosary to be contemplated, e.g., "The Agony in the Garden," along with any special intentions (e.g., for a sick relative, or for an end to war, etc.).

6. On the first large bead before the decade, pray the Our Father.

7. Say a Hail Mary for each of the ten small beads that make up the decade.

8. At the end of the decade, pray the Glory Be.

9. Some Catholics will add optional prayers at the end of each decade, such as the Fatima Prayer (see page 52).

10. Repeat steps 6 through 10 for each of the remaining decades of the Rosary.

11. After completing the fifth decade, many Catholics pray the Hail, Holy Queen (page 53), the Canticle of Mary (page 78), or other additional prayers.

12. Conclude with the Sign of the Cross.

MYSTERIES OF THE ROSARY

The "mysteries" of the Rosary refer to particular events in the life of Jesus and Mary that reveal the saving work of God, who is normally beyond human comprehension. Here are the mysteries of the rosary:

The Joyful Mysteries

1. The Annunciation
The angel Gabriel announces that Mary is to bear God's Son.

2. The Visitation
Mary visits her cousin Elizabeth, who is pregnant with John the Baptist, and the two women praise God for his saving work.

3. The Nativity
Jesus is born, and God comes to meet humanity "in the flesh."

4. The Presentation
Mary and Joseph present Jesus to God in the Temple.

5. The Finding of Jesus in the Temple

After searching for the child Jesus for three days, Mary and Joseph find him among the teachers in the Temple.

The Luminous Mysteries

1. The Baptism of Jesus in the River Jordan

John baptizes Jesus, who is revealed to be God's beloved Son.

2. The Wedding Feast at Cana

In a prefiguring of the Eucharist, Jesus turns water into wine at the request of his mother.

3. The Proclamation of the Kingdom of God

Through his preaching, Jesus calls people to conversion so that God might reign in their lives.

4. The Transfiguration of Jesus

Jesus' glory is revealed to Peter, James, and John.

5. The Institution of the Eucharist

Jesus offers his body and blood for the salvation of the world at the Last Supper.

The Sorrowful Mysteries

1. The Agony in the Garden

Jesus prays in the garden of Gethsemane on the night of his arrest.

2. The Scourging at the Pillar

Pontius Pilate has Jesus whipped.

3. The Crowning with Thorns

Roman soldiers mock Jesus as "king of the Jews" by crowning him with thorns.

4. The Carrying of the Cross

Jesus carries the cross to the place of his crucifixion.

5. The Crucifixion

Jesus is nailed to the cross and dies.

The Glorious Mysteries

1. The Resurrection

Jesus rises from the dead.

2. The Ascension

Jesus returns to his Father in heaven.

3. The Descent of the Holy Spirit at Pentecost

The Holy Spirit descends on the disciples, gathered in the upper room with Mary, and the Church is born.

4. The Assumption of Mary

Mary is assumed into heaven, body and soul.

5. The Coronation of Mary

Mary is crowned as queen of heaven and earth.

MODIFYING THE ROSARY FOR YOUNG CHILDREN

1. Don't use beads, or use kid-friendly ones.
2. Pray just one decade of the rosary.
3. Say only say three Hail Mary prayers for each mystery.
4. Use sacred art to aid meditation.

"Without (contemplation) the Rosary is a body without a soul, and its recitation is in danger of becoming a mechanical repetition of formulas and of going counter to the warning of Christ: 'And in praying do not heap up empty phrases as the Gentiles do; for they think that they will be heard for their many words' (Mt. 6:7). By its nature the recitation of the Rosary calls for a quiet rhythm and a lingering pace, helping the individual to meditate on the mysteries of the Lord's life as seen through the eyes of her who was closest to the Lord. In this way the unfathomable riches of these mysteries are unfolded." (*Pope Paul VI, Marialis Cultus* 47)

Chaplet of Divine Mercy

This prayer is typically said with the aid of rosary beads. Make the Sign of the Cross; then say the Lord's Prayer (Our Father), the Hail Mary (once), and the Apostles' Creed. For each of the five sets of beads, on the large bead, say:

ETERNAL FATHER, I offer you the body and blood, soul and divinity of your dearly beloved Son, our Lord Jesus Christ, in atonement for our sins and those of the whole world.

On each of the ten smaller beads, say:

For the sake of his sorrowful passion, have mercy on us
and on the whole world. After reciting this set of prayers five times (on all five decades), conclude by saying the following prayer three times:

Holy God, Holy Mighty One, Holy Immortal One, have mercy on us and on the whole world.

End by making the Sign of the Cross.

This prayer was given to Saint Faustina Kowalska, a sister of the Congregation of the Sisters of Our Lady of Mercy, in a vision of Jesus in 1935. It may be prayed with the image of Divine Mercy on hand as an object of meditation.

"Blessed are the merciful, for they will receive mercy." (Matthew 5:7)

Meditation and Contemplation

The Church identifies three major expressions of prayer: vocal prayer, meditation, and contemplative prayer (Catechism 2700–2724). Entire libraries of books have been written about meditation and contemplation, and countless individuals have spent their lives practicing these forms of prayer. A full discussion of meditative and contemplative prayer is beyond the scope of this book, but these prayer styles are "bookmarked" here because they are essential to a mature Christian faith.

God is the friend of silence. See how nature—trees and flowers and grass— grows in silence. See the stars, the moon, and the sun, how they move in silence. The more we receive in silent prayer, the more we can give in our active life.

—St. Teresa of Calcutta

Invocations and Scriptures for Meditation

INVOCATIONS AND SHORT SCRIPTURES

The following invocations and bits of Scripture may be repeated silently during a period of meditation. (See *Catechism* 2665–2668.)

Jesus

Son of God

Word of God

Good Shepherd

Lord, come to my assistance. Lord, make haste to help me.

Lord Jesus Christ, Son of God, have mercy on me, a sinner.

Come, Lord Jesus! (Revelation 22:20)

I put my trust in you. (Psalm 56:3)

I give you thanks, O Lord, with my whole heart. (Psalm 138:1)

I praise you, for I am fearfully and wonderfully made. (Psalm 139:14)

This is the day that the Lord has made; let us be glad and rejoice in it. (Psalm 118:24)

Give thanks to the Lord, for he is good, for his steadfast love endures forever. (Psalm 136:1)

"I believe; help my unbelief." (Mark 9:24)

"Here am I, the servant of the Lord; let it be with me according to your word." (Luke 1:38)

"My soul magnifies the Lord." (Luke 1:46–55)

"Jesus, remember me when you come into your kingdom." (Luke 23:42)

"Father, into your hands I commit my spirit." (Luke 23:46)

"My Lord and my God!" (John 20:28)

"I can do all things through him who strengthens me." (Philippians 4:13)

LONGER SCRIPTURES

Here are some texts for *lectio divina* or imaginative prayer.

The Annunciation (Luke 1:26–38): "Do not be afraid, Mary, for you have found favor with God."

The Annunciation to the shepherds (Luke 2:8–20): But the angel said to them, "Do not be afraid; for see—I am bringing you good news of great joy for all the people...."

The boy Jesus in the temple (Luke 2:41–52): When his parents saw him they were astonished....

Jesus is tempted in the desert (Luke 4:1–13): Jesus, full of the Holy Spirit, returned from the Jordan and was led by the Spirit in the wilderness....

The proclamation of the Kingdom (Mark 1:14–15): "The time is fulfilled, and the kingdom of God has come near; repent, and believe in the good news."

Jesus calls the first disciples (Luke 5:1–11): When he had finished speaking, he said to Simon, "Put out into the deep water and let down your nets for a catch."

The wedding at Cana (John 2:1–12): His mother said to the servants, "Do whatever he tells you."

Love of enemies (Luke 6:27–36): Be merciful, just as your Father is merciful.

Parable of the Good Samaritan (Luke 10:25–37): "Which of these three, do you think, was a neighbor to the man who fell into the hands of the robbers?"

Jesus feeds five thousand (Matthew 14:14–21): And all ate and were filled....

Mary and Martha (Luke 10:38–42): "Lord, do you not care that my sister has left me to do all the work by myself?"

Jesus invites Peter to walk on water (Matthew 14:22–33): Peter answered him, "Lord, if it is you, command me to come to you on the water."

Jesus blesses the children (Mark 10:13–16): "Truly I tell you, whoever does not receive the kingdom of God as a little child will never enter it."

The healing of Blind Bartimaeus (Mark 10:46–52): Then Jesus said to him, "What do you want me to do for you?" The blind man said to him, "My teacher, let me see again."

Jesus calms the stormy sea (Luke 8:22–25): A windstorm swept down on the lake, and the boat was filling with water, and they were in danger.

The Crucifixion (Mark 15:21–39): "My God, my God, why have you forsaken me?"

Do not worry (Matthew 6:25–39): "Therefore I tell you, do not worry about your life, what you will eat [or drink], or about your body, what you will wear...."

The Lord will save (Isaiah 43:2–7): ...you are precious in my eyes / and honored, and I love you...

Hope in the Lord (Psalm 43:3–5): O send out your light and your truth / let them lead me...

The work of the Holy Spirit (Philippians 1:6): I am confident of this, that the one who began a good work among you will bring it to completion by the day of Jesus Christ.

Divine majesty and human dignity (Psalm 8): ...what are human beings that you are mindful of them, / mortals that you care for them?

Waiting for divine rescue (Psalm 130): Out of the depths I cry to you, O Lord.

Christian Meditation

MEDITATION is a prayerful quest for God "engaging thought, imagination, emotion, and desire" (*Catechism* 2723). We go out and seek God, usually by focusing our thoughts on some object: a Scripture text (as in lectio divina and imaginative prayer), a mystery of faith (as in the Rosary), sacred art (such as a sacred icon), or even the natural world. Prayerful meditation is different from intellectual study or analysis of the Scripture, artwork, mystery of faith, or whatever the object of meditation might be. It is different because its goal is not to understand, grasp, or intellectually "possess" the object, but to use it as a sort of doorway through which one passes in order to meet God.

The meditation that follows is a method that has been practiced by Christian masters of prayer throughout the history of the Church. For other methods of meditation, see Lectio Divina, Imaginative Prayer, and Meditation on Sacred Art in the following pages, as well as the Rosary (page 52).

Plan on meditating for about five minutes with younger children (beginning about age five) and fifteen minutes with older children and teens.

Begin in this way:

1. Invite your family to choose an invocation to silently repeat throughout the meditation (see the list on page 61). Or suggest the invocation: **"Come, Lord Jesus."**

2. Invite your family to assume a comfortable (but respectful) posture, and to relax their bodies and minds.

3. Begin with a Call to Prayer (page 8).

4. Use these or similar words to begin the period of meditation:

Let's close our eyes and begin our meditation.

Silently repeat the invocation in your heart. It may help to picture Jesus, the Trinity, or some other divine or holy figure.

If you realize that you have stopped saying your invocation because your mind has wandered from your prayer, don't worry. Simply begin saying the invocation again.

If you feel engulfed in the presence of God, you may feel prompted to stop saying your invocation. That's okay; just give yourself over to God's presence.

We'll meditate for about ___ minutes; I will let you know when our time of prayer is finished.

At the end of your period of prayer, close with a short prayer of thanksgiving and the Sign of the Cross.

"The best form of prayer is one that . . . makes space for the presence of God within us." *(St. Basil the Great)*

Contemplation

WHILE meditation uses some holy object as a doorway to God's presence, contemplation might be described as entering that presence; it is an intimate communion with the Lord.

Contemplative prayer is "a gaze of faith, fixed on Jesus," says the *Catechism of the Catholic Church*, which quotes a French peasant who described it in this way: "I look at him, and he looks at me" (2715). Contemplation is both the simplest form of prayer and also the most intense, grounding our being in love (2713, 2714). It is a gift that can only be received in humility (2713). It is the prayer of silence, with few or no words (2717).

How can you practice contemplative prayer as a family? Because it is a gift, it is not something you can "do." But you can make your children aware of what it is, and you can create conditions that are favorable to entering contemplative prayer. Generally, contemplative prayer begins with and emerges from meditation; the method of meditation described on page 62 is one way to begin. You may also find it helpful to light a candle, display an icon of Jesus, or take your children to Eucharistic adoration.

"When picturing Christ in the way I have mentioned, or sometimes even when reading, I used unexpectedly to experience a consciousness of the presence of God, of such a kind that I could not possibly doubt that he was within me or that I was wholly engulfed in him. This was in no sense a vision: I believe it is called mystical theology. The soul is suspended in such a way that it seems to be completely outside itself. The will loves; the memory, I think, is almost lost; while the understanding, I believe, though it is not lost, does not reason—I mean that it does not work, but is amazed at the extent of all it can understand; for God wills it to realize that it understands nothing of what his majesty represents to it. This is a favor neither wholly of sense, nor wholly of spirit, but entirely the gift of God." *(St. Teresa of Avila)*

Lectio Divina

LECTIO DIVINA ("sacred reading") is an ancient method of praying with sacred texts that dates to the fourth century. Usually the sacred text comes from the Scriptures, but other texts may be used as well. The basic idea is to spend time listening deeply and intently to what God might have to say to you through the text—almost as if the sacred text were a much-cherished love letter from God.

Lectio divina is traditionally divided into four steps: *lectio* (reading), *meditatio* (meditation), *oratio* (prayer), and *contemplatio* (contemplation). These steps do not need to be followed exactly in order; you may feel prompted to move between them fluidly.

Choosing Texts

Use one of the readings from the day's Mass or Liturgy of the Hours as your text, or choose a favorite text of your own, or consult the list under "Invocations and Scriptures for Meditation" (page 59). Young children may do *lectio* from a book of Bible stories.

Lectio Divina for the Family

BEGIN with the Sign of the Cross and silence.

IN THE NAME of the Father, and the Son, and the Holy Spirit. Holy Spirit, you inspired the authors of Sacred Scripture to write what you wanted us to know for the sake of our salvation. Inspire us now to hear those words not only with our ears, but our hearts, so that we might know your saving Word for us today. *Silence.*

READ the sacred text several times. Introduce this step with these or similar words:

Listen to this reading carefully, paying attention to what words, images, or ideas the Holy Spirit brings to your heart.

Read the sacred text slowly, savoring the words and pausing briefly after significant phrases and sentences. Observe a brief silence after the first reading.

Read the sacred text again (or ask someone else to do so), observing a brief silence afterward. If appropriate, pause to discuss the meaning of the text, using footnotes and commentaries as needed.

Read the text a third time, and observe a brief silence.

MEDITATE. In the meditation step, ask questions such as:

What words, images, or ideas did the Holy Spirit bring to your heart? What stood out for you in the reading?

How do those words, images, or ideas relate to your life right now?

What might God be saying to you (us) in this reading? What action might you (we) be called to take?

How does God's word make you feel? Excited, encouraged, comforted, loved? Or do you feel challenged, confused, or resistant?

Offer your own reflection as a model before inviting your children to share their own thoughts.

PRAY. Respond to the reading by addressing God in prayer. Say:

Let's respond to God's word for us in prayer.

Exactly how you pray the reading will depend on what surfaced during the meditation step. Some possibilities:

- Offer thanksgiving to God for important insights that emerged from the text.
- If the text was difficult or confusing, ask God for guidance and clarity.
- If the text was challenging or caused anxiety, ask God for humility, strength, and the ability to trust in providence.

CONTEMPLATE. Invite family members to still themselves and "rest in the Word," attending to God's presence:

Let's quiet our hearts for a few moments so we might hear God's response to our prayer. Rest now in God's presence.

CLOSE. After a period of silence, end with the Sign of the Cross:

IN THE NAME **of the Father, and the Son, and the Holy Spirit.**

"For ignorance of the Scriptures is ignorance of Christ." *(Dei Verbum 25)*

Imaginative Prayer

AS THE NAME suggests, imaginative prayer puts the imagination at the disposal of the Holy Spirit, so that the imagination becomes a way of speaking to God and hearing God speak to us. It was popularized by St. Ignatius of Loyola, who learned it by reading the German theologian Ludolph of Saxony.

Imaginative prayer is usually rooted in a sacred text—usually a visually appealing, detailed story from the Bible, although St. Ignatius also used stories from the lives of the saints as an object of meditation. The basic method involves placing oneself inside the story, either as one of the characters or as an onlooker. The imagination supplies details not provided by the original text, including sensory details such as smells, sounds, sights, and tastes. The meditation may lead to a conversation or interaction with one of the main characters—perhaps Jesus or Mary, or another holy figure. Alternatively, the pray-er may use the imaginative experience to simply enter God's presence.

Use the following steps as a basic guide in leading your family in imaginative prayer.

1. If your family is new to imaginative prayer, briefly describe it and preview these steps.

2. Choose a story, either from the Bible, a book of children's Bible stories, or a book of saint stories. Choose a dynamic story, one with a bit of action in it. The list on page 60 may be helpful.

3. Invite your family to assume a comfortable (but respectful) posture, and to relax their bodies and minds.

4. Begin with a Call to Prayer (page 8).

5. Prayerfully read the story out loud once or twice, slowly and prayerfully. It may be helpful for older family members to have

a copy of the story available for them to read during the period of prayer.

6.   Pray with these or similar words:

Lord, you made us in your image with creative and imaginative minds. Send your Holy Spirit now so that by our imagination, we might enter your presence.

Optionally, guide the meditation with these prompts:

Imagine the scene. What do you see? What do you hear and smell? What do you feel? What is the weather like? What is happening around you?

Observe a period of silence.

Place yourself as a person in the scene. Who are you?

Observe a period of silence.

Let the action of the story unfold, participating and interacting with people in the story as you like.

Observe a period of silence.

7.   Close your time of prayer with the Sign of the Cross.

Spend some time after your time of prayer reflecting on the experience, either together or individually. What happened? What feelings or emotions did you experience? What do your emotions or your actions reveal about you? What might God be saying to you?

"Pick up the Gospel, select a passage, read it once, read it twice; imagine, as if you see what is happening, and contemplate Jesus . . . . And in this way, your knowledge of Jesus will be greater and your hope will grow." (*Pope Francis*)

An Examination of Conscience

This brief examination of conscience, loosely based on the Ten Commandments, may be used in preparation for receiving the sacrament of penance and reconciliation, or as a kind of daily examen. Your family may wish to review it together silently, or with the guidance of a reader.

HAVE I made anything more important than God: myself, others, money, things I own, things I want, ideas, activities, or goals? Have I set aside time to pray to God every day?

Have I acted pridefully, as if I know everything, am better than others, or don't need God or others?

Have I used God's name in a bad way? Have my words hurt God, his Church, or the good he wants for all people? Have my words and actions given glory to God's name? Have I shared my faith with those who do not know God?

Have I gone to Mass when I should? Have I fully shared in the celebration of Mass? Have I listened to the Word of God and the homily? Have I received the Eucharist reverently?

Have I spent my Sundays in prayer, rest, service, and family time?

Have I given love and respect to my father and mother? Have I obeyed them? Have I tried to help them without being asked? Have I whined, complained, nagged, or otherwise been difficult toward them?

Have I been loving and respectful to my brothers and sisters?

Parents: Have I shown love and respect to my children? Have I been patient and kind? Have I disciplined my children with love, and in ways that help them become the people God wants them to be?

Have I been a good citizen? Have my words and actions strengthened my community, or harmed it?

Have I hurt others, with my hands or my words? Have I given support or encouragement to those who hurt others? Have I excluded others, or treated others with less than the respect they deserve as children of God? Have I held onto anger or hatred toward others? Have I refused to forgive others?

Have I respected my body? Have I given my body what it needs to be strong and healthy? Have I viewed pornography, engaged in sexual acts outside of marriage, or otherwise offended
human dignity for my own pleasure?

Have I taken what does not belong to me? Have I wasted time or resources? Have I used my talents and resources to help those in need? Have I let others borrow my possessions for good reason?

Have I done my work well? Have I contributed to the good of others through my work? Have I done my chores and school-work as best I can, with a good attitude?

Have I always told the truth to myself, God, and others? Have I gossiped, or shared information I shouldn't have?

Have I been grateful for what I have, or greedy to have what others have? Have I been generous with my time and possessions? Have I given away what I do not need?

"Return to your conscience, question it…. Turn inward, brethren, and in everything you do, see God as your witness." *(St. Augustine)*

Praying with Sacred Art

CHRISTIANS *have long used sacred art—art that is directed toward God, or holy things—as an object for meditation. As with other objects of meditation, the ultimate goal is to pass beyond the artwork itself, using it as a doorway to God's presence. The method presented here is divided into three parts: seeing, meditating, and responding.*

The following process may be directed by a prayer leader, or done individually.

1. Make the Sign of the Cross.

2. If the artwork depicts a biblical scene, read the relevant Bible passage.

3. Observe a period of silence simply gazing at the picture.

4. See. Begin by considering the following questions:

   What is the artwork about?

   What details do you notice?

   What is the mood of the artwork?

   What are the people in the artwork doing? What do their postures and facial expressions say about their feelings?

5. Meditate. Briefly call on the Holy Spirit to inspire you as you consider how God might be speaking to you through the artwork. Consider the following questions:

   Which figure do you most identify with? Why?

   Does the artist's depiction of the subject affirm or challenge the way you thought of the subject previously?

   If you were the artist, how would you paint the subject differently, and why?

If you were painted into the artwork, what would you look like? Where would you be, and what would you be doing?

How is God present or active in the artwork?

What feelings does the art surface in you? What events or issues in your life does it bring to mind?

6.   Respond to the artwork in silent prayer.

Let us spend several minutes in the presence of the Lord. During this time, consider what God might be saying to you, and what you might want to say to God.

7.   After a few moments of silence, end with the Sign of the Cross.

"Created 'in the image of God' (Genesis 1:26), man also expresses the truth of his relationship with God the Creator by the beauty of his artistic works. Sacred art is true and beautiful when its form corresponds to its particular vocation: evoking and glorifying, in faith and adoration, the transcendent mystery of God—the surpassing invisible beauty of truth and love visible in Christ, who 'reflects the glory of God and bears the very stamp of his nature,' in whom 'the whole fullness of deity dwells bodily' (Hebrews 1:3; Colossians 2:9)." *(Catechism 2501–2502)*

Evening Prayer

St. Paul urged the earliest Christians to "pray constantly" (1 Thessalonians 5:17). Over the centuries, the Church developed a way to pray at regular intervals throughout the day. This traditional practice is known as the Liturgy of the Hours, or the Divine Office. The Liturgy of the Hours is like an extension of the celebration of Mass into everyday life, a way for Christians to sanctify the day.

Evening Prayer, also called Vespers, is one of the major "hours" in the Liturgy of the Hours. While it may be impractical to formally pray the full Office daily, many families "bookend" their day with morning and evening prayers.

The following evening prayers offer a simple way for your family to gather up the events of the day and bring them to God...and to ask for his peace and protection during the night.

Daily Examen

An Examen for Younger Children

For children ages five through nine, talk through the examen using this shortened method.

ENTER God's presence.

Leader: **Let's pray about our day.**
Make the Sign of the Cross.

**God, you have been with us all day long,
since the time we woke up until now; help us
to remember our day, so we can bring it to you.**

REVIEW the day.

Review the events of the day, moving through the parts of the day and offering prompts as necessary. For example:

Leader: **What happened in the morning when we woke up?…
What happened at school? … When we got home? … When
were we angry? … Sad? … Happy? … What was beautiful? …
What was amazing?**

DISCERN God's presence in the events of the day.

Leader: **How was God present to us today?**

Look for God's presence, not only in moments of happiness, but also in the difficult, sad, or challenging events of the day.

Leader: **How did we respond to God's presence? When were
we loving? When were we not loving?**

PRAY the day. Invite your family to think about what Jesus is saying to them through the events of the day. For example:

Leader: **What do you think Jesus says about our day?**

Invite them to pray in response.

Leader: **What do we want to tell Jesus about our day?**

Encourage prayers of praise, thankfulness, repentance, and the grace to draw closer to God. Close with the Sign of the Cross.

An Examen for Older Children and Teens

Older children and teens may like to write down their responses to the various prompts in a prayer journal. As you lead this simplified version of the examen, briefly describe each step, allowing several minutes of silent reflection for each one.

ENTER God's presence. Take a few moments to quiet down, to recall that God has accompanied you every step of the way during the day, and to open yourself to God's presence.

REVIEW the events of the day in a spirit of gratitude. Move through your day, hour by hour, taking special note of its many small gifts: the warmth of a child's hand, the taste of good food, a flock of birds, the kindness of a stranger. Recall that God is revealed in each of these details. Think, too, about the gifts you were able to give others: a smile, work well done, etc.

PRAY for the Spirit of truth. Prepare for the next step by asking for the Spirit of truth to "guide you into all truth" (John 16:13). Prepare yourself to be honest as you examine your day, knowing that the truth will free you to grow closer to God. Recall, too, God's unconditional love for you.

EXAMINE how you responded (or not) to God's presence in the key events of the day. When were you loving? When did you miss a chance to love? When were you sinful? How much were you in charge of your actions, and what did you do out of simple habit? Pay attention to your emotions around these events. St. Ignatius taught that the Holy Spirit often speaks to us through our emotions, even the "negative" ones. What truth might God be revealing to you through your emotions?

RESPOND in prayer to the insights revealed in the previous steps. You may want to imagine this as a friendly face-to-face meeting with Jesus, one in which you offer words of sorrow, gratitude, or joy. You may want to ask for forgiveness, consolation, encouragement, the grace to overcome bad habits, and direction for how to grow closer to God. When you are finished, close your prayer with the Sign of the Cross, and continue to listen to Jesus throughout the rest of your day.

A daily examen is a prayerful method of "checking in" on how well we are living out our Christian faith on a daily basis. Developed by St. Ignatius of Loyola more than four hundred years ago, the examen invites us to reflect on how God has been present in our day, how we have responded to that presence, and how we might grow in holiness.

Canticle of Mary (Magnificat)

MY SOUL proclaims the greatness of the Lord,
my spirit rejoices in God my Savior
for he has looked with favor on his lowly servant.

From this day all generations will call me blessed:
the Almighty has done great things for me,
and holy is his name.

He has mercy on those who fear him
in every generation.

He has shown the strength of his arm,
he has scattered the proud in their conceit.

He has cast down the mighty from their thrones,
and has lifted up the lowly.

He has filled the hungry with good things,
and the rich he has sent away empty.

He has come to the help of his servant Israel
for he has remembered his promise of mercy,
the promise he made to our fathers,
to Abraham and his children for ever.

Glory to the Father, and to the Son, and to the Holy Spirit:
as it was in the beginning, is now, and will be forever.

Amen.

Mary's psalm of praise is found in Luke 1:46–55, and is the longest speech of Mary in the Bible. This prayer of humility and gratitude invites us to imitate Mary by "bringing forth" Christ in our own lives.

Canticle of Simeon

LORD now you let your servant go in peace;
your word has been fulfilled.
My eyes have seen the salvation
you have prepared in the sight of every people,
a light to reveal you to the nations
and the glory of your people, Israel.

Glory to the Father, and to the Son, and to the Holy Spirit:
as it was in the beginning, is now, and will be forever.

Amen.

The prayer of Simeon upon viewing the child Jesus in the Temple is
recorded in Luke 2:29–32. It is also known as the Nunc Dimittis, and
has been sung as part of Evening or Night Prayer since the fourth
century.

Phos Hilaron

O RADIANT light, O sun divine
of God the Father's deathless face,
O image of the light sublime
that fills the heavenly dwelling place.

O Son of God, the source of life,
praise is your due by night and day;
unsullied lips must raise the strain
of your proclaimed and splendid name.

Lord Jesus Christ, as daylight fades,
as shine the lights of eventide,
we praise the Father with the Son,
the Spirit blest and with them one.

Phos Hilaron is the earliest known Christian hymn, recorded in the
Apostolic Constitutions in the fourth century. The hymn was to be
sung at the lighting of lamps in the evening, which is why it is sometimes known as the lamp-lighting hymn.

Canticle of the Three Youths (Daniel 3:57–90 NABRE)

This prayer might be said antiphonally, with a leader speaking the verses and all responding on "praise and exalt him above all forever."

BLESS the Lord, all you works of the Lord,
  praise and exalt him above all forever.
Angels of the Lord, bless the Lord,
  praise and exalt him above all forever.
You heavens, bless the Lord,
  praise and exalt him above all forever.
All you waters above the heavens, bless the Lord,
  praise and exalt him above all forever.
All you powers, bless the Lord;
  praise and exalt him above all forever.
Sun and moon, bless the Lord;
  praise and exalt him above all forever.
Stars of heaven, bless the Lord;
  praise and exalt him above all forever.
Every shower and dew, bless the Lord;
  praise and exalt him above all forever.
All you winds, bless the Lord;
  praise and exalt him above all forever.
Fire and heat, bless the Lord;
  praise and exalt him above all forever.
Cold and chill, bless the Lord;
  praise and exalt him above all forever.
Dew and rain, bless the Lord;
  praise and exalt him above all forever.
Frost and chill, bless the Lord;
  praise and exalt him above all forever.

Hoarfrost and snow, bless the Lord;
praise and exalt him above all forever.
Nights and days, bless the Lord;
praise and exalt him above all forever.
Light and darkness, bless the Lord;
praise and exalt him above all forever.
Lightnings and clouds, bless the Lord;
praise and exalt him above all forever.
Let the earth bless the Lord,
praise and exalt him above all forever.
Mountains and hills, bless the Lord;
praise and exalt him above all forever.
Everything growing on earth, bless the Lord;
praise and exalt him above all forever.
You springs, bless the Lord;
praise and exalt him above all forever.
Seas and rivers, bless the Lord;
praise and exalt him above all forever.
You sea monsters and all water creatures,
bless the Lord;
praise and exalt him above all forever.
All you birds of the air, bless the Lord;
praise and exalt him above all forever.
All you beasts, wild and tame, bless the Lord;
praise and exalt him above all forever.
All you mortals, bless the Lord;
praise and exalt him above all forever.
O Israel, bless the Lord;
praise and exalt him above all forever.
Priests of the Lord, bless the Lord;
praise and exalt him above all forever.

Servants of the Lord, bless the Lord;
  praise and exalt him above all forever.
Spirits and souls of the just, bless the Lord;
  praise and exalt him above all forever.
Holy and humble of heart, bless the Lord;
  praise and exalt him above all forever.
Hananiah, Azariah, Mishael, bless the Lord;
  praise and exalt him above all forever.
For he has delivered us from Sheol,
  and saved us from the power of death;
He has freed us from the raging flame
  and delivered us from the fire.
Give thanks to the Lord, who is good,
  whose mercy endures forever.
Bless the God of gods, all you who fear the Lord;
  praise and give thanks,
  for his mercy endures forever.

This is the hymn sung by the three youths from within the fiery furnace that King Nebuchadnezzar had them thrown into as a punishment for refusing to worship his idol (Daniel 3). It is omitted from most Protestant Bibles on the grounds that it was written in Greek rather than the Aramaic of the rest of the book of Daniel.

Watch, O Lord

WATCH, O Lord,
with those who wake, or watch, or weep tonight,
and give your angels charge over those who sleep.

Tend your sick ones, O Lord Christ.

Rest your weary ones.

Bless your dying ones.

Soothe your suffering ones.

Pity your afflicted ones.

Shield your joyous ones.

And for all your love's sake.

Amen.

This prayer was composed by St. Augustine (354–430).

Children's Bedside Prayer

BLESS me, Lord, as this day ends,
Bless my family and all my friends,
Keep me safe throughout the night,
and wake me with the morning's light.

Now I Lay Me Down to Sleep

NOW I lay me down to sleep,
I pray the Lord my soul to keep.
Angels watch me through the night,
And wake me with the morning light.

Pope Francis's Five-Finger Prayer

1. The thumb is the closest finger to you. So start praying for those who are closest to you. They are the persons easiest to remember. To pray for our dear ones is a "sweet obligation."

2. The next finger is the index finger. Pray for those who teach you, instruct you, and heal you. They need God's help as they offer direction for others.

3. The following finger is the tallest. It reminds us of our government leaders and others who have authority. They need God's guidance.

4. The fourth finger is the ring finger, which is also our weakest finger. It should remind us to pray for the weakest among us—the sick, the poor, those excluded from society, and those plagued by other problems.

5. And finally we have our smallest finger, the smallest of all. Your pinkie should remind you to pray for yourself. When you are done praying for the other four groups, you will be able to pray for your own needs in a better way.

Pope Francis composed this prayer for children during the time that he was the archbishop of Buenos Aires, Argentina.

Psalm 23

THE LORD is my shepherd, I shall not want.
He makes me lie down in green pastures;
he leads me beside still waters;
  he restores my soul.

He leads me in right paths
  for his name's sake.
Even though I walk through
the darkest valley,
  I fear no evil;
for you are with me;
  your rod and your staff—
    they comfort me.
You prepare a table before me
  in the presence of my enemies;
you anoint my head with oil;
  my cup overflows.

Surely goodness and mercy shall follow me
  all the days of my life,
and I shall dwell in the house of the Lord
  my whole life long.
  ✠

This psalm compares God to a shepherd who protects and cares for his sheep, and as a host whose generosity "overflows." Christians see in this psalm a connection to Jesus under the figure of the Good Shepherd (John 10:11–18).

Acknowledgments

Unless otherwise noted, Scripture quotations in this work are from New Revised Standard Version Bible: Catholic Edition, copyright © 1989, 1993 National Council of the Churches of Christ in the United States of America. Used by permission. All rights reserved worldwide.

Scripture texts in this work indicated with the abbreviation NABRE are taken from the New American Bible, revised edition © 2010, 1991, 1986, 1970 Confraternity of Christian Doctrine, Washington, D.C. and are used by permission of the copyright owner. All Rights Reserved. No part of the New American Bible may be reproduced in any form without permission in writing from the copyright owner.

The English translation of "Come, Holy Spirit" from *A Book of Prayers* © 1982, International Commission on English in the Liturgy Corporation (ICEL); the "Apostles' Creed," "Gloria in Excelsis Deo (Great Doxology)" and "Confiteor" are excerpted from the English translation of The Roman Missal © 2010, ICEL. All rights reserved.

Quotes from the *Catechism of the Catholic Church* are taken from the English translation of the *Catechism of the Catholic Church for the United States of America*, 2nd ed. Copyright 1997 by United States Catholic Conference—Libreria Editrice Vaticana.

"Blessed are You, Lord" from *A Book of Blessings*, copyright © Concacan Inc., 1981; "Prayer after meals" from *Blessings and Prayers for Home and Family*, © Concacan Inc., 2004. All rights reserved. Reproduced with permission of the Canadian Conference of Catholic Bishops. Visit cccbpublications.ca.

English translations of "Glory Be to the Father" (page 22), "Te Deum" (page 26) "Canticle of Zechariah" (page 12), "Canticle of Mary" (page 78), "Canticle of Simeon" (page 79), © 1988 English Language Liturgical Consultation (ELLC). www.englishtexts.org. Used by permission.

Prayers

The following prayers and articles are by Jerry Windley-Daoust: "Children's Call to Prayer" (page 8), "A Short Morning Offering for Children" (page 12), "Consecration to the Holy Family" (page 31), "Intercessory Prayers" (pages 33–34), "Giving Thanks" (page 35), "Blessing of Persons" (page 38), "Blessing of an Object" (page 39), "Blessing for Someone Who Is Sick" (page 40), "The Rosary" (page 52), "Invocations and Scriptures for Meditation" (page 59), "Christian Meditation" (page 62), "Contemplation" (page 64), "Lectio Divina" (page 65), "Imaginative Prayer" (page 68), "An Examination of Conscience" (page 70), "Praying with Sacred Art (page 72), "Daily Examen" (page 75). All rights reserved.

All other prayers are believed to be in the public domain unless noted below.

"Morning Offering" (page 14) is by Fr. François-Xavier Gautrelet as quoted in *Catholic Household Blessings and Prayers*, p. 48 (USCCB Publishing, 2007). All rights reserved.

"Gloria in Excelsis Deo (Great Doxology)" (page 23) is excerpted from the English translation of The Roman Missal © 2010, ICEL. All rights reserved.

"Confiteor" (page 24) is excerpted from the English translation of The Roman Missal © 2010, ICEL. All rights reserved.

"Come, Holy Spirit" (page 25) is from *A Book of Prayers* © 1982, International Commission on English in the Liturgy Corporation (ICEL). "Te Deum Laudamus" (page 26) is from the 1975 ICET version accessed at "Te Deum Laudamus" at Britannica.

com."Blessed Are You, Lord" (page 43) is from *A Book of Blessings*, copyright © Concacan Inc., 1981. All rights reserved. Reproduced with permission of the Canadian Conference of Catholic Bishops. Visit cccbpublications.ca.

"Prayer after Meals" (page 43) is from *Blessings and Prayers for Home and Family*, © Concacan Inc., 2004. All rights reserved. Reproduced with permission of the Canadian Conference of Catholic Bishops. Visit cccbpublications.ca.

Quotations

The quote from St. Thérèse of Lisieux on page 7 is from her *Story of a Soul,* as quoted in the *Catechism of Catholic Church* 2559.

The quote from John Baptist de La Salle on page 9 is from his *Explanation of the Method of Interior Prayer* as translated by Donald Mouton, FSC (Lasallian Publications, 1995).

The quote from Tertullian on page 9 is from his *De Corona* as quoted in *The Cross Before Constantine: The Early Life of a Christian Symbol* by Bruce W. Longenecker (Fortress Press, 2015).

The quote from St. Pope John XXIII on page 19 is taken from *Our Different Gifts* by Bernadette Stankard (Twenty-third Publications, 2013).

The quote from Clement of Alexandria on page 19 is from his *Miscellaneous Studies,* as quoted in *The Quotable Saint* by Rosemary Guiley (Facts on File, 2002).

The quote from St. Josemaria Escriva on page 19 is quoted from multiple sources online; the original source is unknown.

The quote from John Climacus on page 40 is from *The Ladder of Divine Ascent,* Step 28.

The quote from St. Teresa of Calcutta on page 58 is from *In the Silence: Meditations* composed by Kathryn Spink (SPCK, 1983), p 19–20.

The quote from St. Basil the Great on page 63 is from his letter to St. Gregory of Nyssa, as quoted in *The Quotable Saint* by Rosemary Guiley (Facts on File, 2002).

The quote from St. Teresa of Avila on page 13 is taken from *The Life of Teresa of Jesus: The Autobiography of St. Teresa of Ávila,* by Teresa of Avila (Image Books, 2004).

The quote from Pope Francis on page 69 is from "Morning Meditation in the Chapel of the Domus Sanctae Marthae" Tuesday 3 February 2015. Accessed at vatican.va.

The quote from St. Augustine on page 71 is from *Homilies on the First Epistle of John* by St. Augustine, translated by Boniface Ramsey and edited by Daniel E. Doyle, O.S.A., and Thomas Martin, O.S.A. (New City Press, 2008), p. 124.

Artworks

Page 3: A detail from the painting *Eucharist in Fruit Wreath,* 1648, by Jan Davidsz de Heem. Used with permission of the Kunsthistorisches Museum, Vienna. • Pages 4, 7, 11, 19, 30, 44, 58, 74: an artwork based on the north rose window in Notre Dame Cathedral, Paris • Page 8: Nativity Star. • Pages 9, 41, and 67: A detail of a jeweled crucifix depicted in Hiberno-Saxon style. • Page 10: Icons of the Gospel writers. • Page 12: A detail of *Simeon's Song of Praise,* circa 1700, by Aert de Geider, Royal Picture Gallery Mauritshuis,

Netherlands. • Page 13: A detail of a fresco painting from the Basilica dei Sainti Apostoli, 1400s, by Melozzo da Forli, Vatican Museums. • Page 14: A stained glass window depicting the Immaculate Heart of Mary. • Page 15: A detail of a painting, *Beloved Saint Francis,* by Jen Norton, www.jennortonartstudio.com. Used with permission. • Page 16: A watercolor of green clover by Issalina, Adobe Stock. • Page 17: A detail of *Christ Enthroned* from the Book of Kells, 700s, Trinity College Library, Dublin. • Page 18: A detail from Saint Luke, c. 1510, by the Workshop of the Master of the First Prayer Book of Maximilian, Flemish, J. Paul Getty Museum, New York. • Page 20: A detail of an icon of the Holy Family of Saint Basil the Great. • Page 21: A detail of children's art by Gisele Bauche, www.baucheart.com/gisele. Used with permission. • Page 22: A detail of a Filipino painting of a mother and child. • Page 23: A detail of a ceiling painting, 1730, by Daniel Gran, Austrian National Library, Vienna. • Page 24: A detail of an oil painting, *The Coronation of the Virgin,* 1635–36, The Prado Museum, Madrid. • Page 25: A detail of an illustration on parchment from *The Hours of Marguerite d'Orleans,* c. 1426, The National Library of France, Paris. • Page 26: A detail of the painting *Starry Night* by Vincent Van Gogh, 1889, Museum of Modern Art, New York. • Page 28: *Mexican Sacred Heart,* by Jackie Gonzalez, www.etsy.com/shop/ArtbyJackieGonzalez. Used with permission. • Page 29: A detail of a stained glass window at St. Michael's Cemetery, 2010, by Pickel Studio, New York. • Page 32: *The Vigin and Child* by Bradi Barth, www.bradi-barth.org. Used with permission. • Pages 34, 78: A watercolor by Guz Anna, Adobe Stock. • Pages 36, 82: A watercolor by wolna_luna, Adobe Stock. • Page 35: A detail of *Tree of Life* by Oscar Steno Elias. • Page 37: A detail of a painting of St. Francis and the animals. • Pages 39, 54, 75, 85: A watercolor by Irina Violet, Adobe Stock. • Page 42: A detail of a stained glass window, *Miracle of the Loaves and Fishes,* c. 1525, by Jan Rombouts, Flemish, The Metropolitan Museum of Art, New York. • Page 45: A detail of a mosiac of Mary. • Page 46: A mosaic of *The Visitation of the Blessed Virgin Mary.* • Page 48: A detail of a painting, *The Trinity,* c. 1635, by José de Ribera, The Prado Museum, Madrid. • Page 51: A detail of *Our Lady of Guadalupe,* 1500s, the Basilica of Our Lady of Guadalupe, Mexico City. • Page 54: A detail of a sculpture of *Our Lady of the Rosary,* the Parish Church of Urtijëi, Italy. • Page 57: *Divine Mercy,* by Eugeniusz Kazimirowski, Divine Mercy Sanctuary of Vilnius, Lithuania. • Page 63: A detail of a ceiling mosaic, *Christus Pantocrator,* the Cathedral of Cefalù, Italy. • Page 67: A detail of a stained glass window depicting the Crucifixion. • Page 73: A painting, *Jesus and the Daughter of Jairus.* • Page 77: A detail of an oil painting, *The Supper at Emmaus,* 1648, by Rembrant Harmenszoon van Rijn, the Louvre Museum, Paris. • Page 79: A detail of a oil painting, *The Circumcision,* c. 1500, Workshop of Giovanni Bellini, The National Gallery, London. • Page 80: A detail from an illumination on parchment from a Missal, c. 1310, East Anglia, the National Library of Wales, Aberystwyth. • Page 83: A detail from an illustration in an Ethiopian psalter of an archangel protecting Shadrach, Meshach, and Abednego in the furnace, 1700s, St. Andrews University, Scotland. • Page 84: A detail of an acrylic painting, *The Shepherds,* 2012, by Sue Hodge, www.visualartist. info/suehodge. Used with permission. • Page 86: A detail of *The Good Shepherd*, by Vicki Shuck. Used with permission.

My Prayers

My Prayers

Prayer Intentions

Prayer Intentions

Faithful Departed

Faithful Departed